THE NIÑA,
THE PINTA,
AND
THE SANTA MARÍA

The Niña, the Pinta, and the Santa María

DENNIS BRINDELL FRADIN

FRANKLIN WATTS

New York • London • Toronto • Sydney
A First Book • 1991

FOR MY FRIEND BOB HANDLER, WITH LOVE

Cover photograph courtesy of Historical Pictures Service, Chicago

Cover design by Karen K. Quigley

Photographs courtesy of: Ronald Sheridan/Ancient Art and
Architecture Collection: pp. 2, 11, 12, 14, 55; New York
Public Library, Picture Collection: p. 8; The Bettmann
Archive: pp. 16, 25, 31, 41, 47; Historical Pictures Service,
Chicago: pp. 18, 22, 26, 37, 39, 43, 50 top, 52; Art Resource
Inc.: pp. 29 (Scala), 33 (Giraudon), 57 (Scala); D. & M.
Zimmerman/Vireo: p. 48; Ampliaciones y Reproducciones Mas
(Arxiu Mas), Barcelona: p. 50 bottom; The Mariners Museum: p. 58.

Library of Congress Cataloging-in-Publication Data

Fradin, Dennis B.
The Niña, the Pinta, and the Santa María/Dennis Brindell
Fradin. p. cm. -- (A First book)
Includes bibliographical references and index.
Summary: A biography of Christopher Columbus, focusing
on his voyage to America aboard the three famous ships.
ISBN 0-531-20034-5
1. Columbus, Christopher—Journeys—Juvenile literature.
2. America—Discovery and exploration—Spanish—Juvenile
literature.
[1. Columbus, Christopher. 2. Explorers. 3. America—
Discovery and exploration—Spanish.] I. Title. II. Series.
E118.F73 1991
970.01'5—dc20   91-4664 CIP AC

CONTENTS

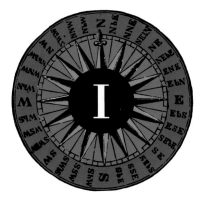

COLUMBUS'S QUEST FOR SHIPS

Sometime in 1485 a man and a boy boarded a ship in Lisbon, Portugal. The man, a thirty-four-year-old sailor named Christopher Columbus, was tall and had red hair and blue eyes. He had endured two misfortunes recently, so perhaps there was a sad look in his eyes as the ship sailed south from Lisbon. His wife had died, and Portugal's king had refused him the ships he needed for a daring voyage. He was now moving to Spain, where he hoped to obtain the ships.

The boy, five-year-old Diego Columbus, was Christopher's son. Diego was old enough to know that his mother was dead and that he and his father were moving to a new country. But he was probably too young to understand his father's almost constant talk about his great dream—a westward voyage to Asia.

*A nineteenth-century painting shows
the vision that inspired Columbus as he
and his son traveled from court to court,
seeking support for his voyage.*

What was the background of this man who talked about his dream voyage so much that other people considered him something of an oddball? Christopher Columbus had been born in the seafaring city of Genoa, Italy, in 1451. Perhaps as early as the age of ten he had gone on his first voyage to a port near Genoa. When not helping his father in his wool-weaving business, Christopher continued to go to sea. By his early twenties, he had begun making longer voyages. Uneducated but bright, Christopher learned a great deal about handling ships and planning routes on these voyages.

A shipboard disaster in 1476 changed the course of Christopher's life. In the summer of that year, he was on a ship that was attacked and sunk off Portugal's coast. Christopher was wounded, but he managed to grab a loose piece of wood and paddle the few miles to shore.

Christopher's brother Bartholomew was already living in Portugal. Bartholomew worked in a map shop in Lisbon, Portugal's capital. The late 1400s were years when European sailors were traveling farther and farther from the continent of Europe. In fact, the period from the late 1400s through the 1500s is known as the Age of Discovery because of all the explorations during that time. Ship captains wanted maps that showed the best sailing routes and what the land was like in far-off places. Bartholomew arranged a job for Christopher in the map shop.

The two brothers would go down to the docks and meet ships that arrived in Lisbon. By speaking to the ship captains, they would learn the latest news about sailing routes and distant lands.

Christopher and Bartholomew eventually opened their own map shop in Lisbon. And now and then Christopher shipped out on expeditions to such places as Ireland, Iceland, and the Madeira Islands, off the coast of Africa.

Sometime in the late 1470s, Christopher Columbus had an idea that greatly excited him. At that time, Europeans wanted to visit China, Japan, and other Asian lands. They sought gold, spices, and other valuable goods in Asia. The overland trip from Europe to Asia was difficult and time-consuming. Nearly everyone thought the best way to reach Asia would be by sailing south and then east around Africa. But such a voyage had never been made before. Each year explorers sailed farther down Africa's coast in the hope of one day making it all the way around to Asia.

At the busy port of fifteenth-century Lisbon, ships were outfitted for voyages of trade and of exploration.

But it wasn't until 1498 that Vasco da Gama led the first European expedition that reached Asia by sailing around Africa.

Christopher Columbus thought that there must be an easier sailing route to Asia, by sailing west across the Atlantic Ocean. From the time of the ancient Greeks, educated people had known that the earth was round, which means that any place can be reached by going east *or* west. Columbus thought that sailing west would be a shorter and easier route than by sailing all the way around Africa to Asia.

Columbus was fascinated by the idea of the westward voyage to Asia. He read every geography book he could find. He figured distances, and how much food and water would be needed. When he married in about 1479, it was to a young woman whose father had been a sea captain. Christopher spent a lot of time studying her father's charts, which increased his desire to make his dream voyage.

Columbus knew that he could not finance his voyage by himself. To start with, he would need several

Mapmakers before the time of Columbus knew the world was round—as shown in this thirteenth-century world map— but much of it was unknown.

Calicu

Vasco da Gama led a fleet of ships in a
two-year voyage around the Cape of Africa
to reach Asia. Here, a sixteenth-century
artist shows him arriving at Calcutta.

ships. If one sank, the others could rescue his men. Dozens of sailors were also needed. And there had to be enough food, water, and supplies to sustain them through the few weeks he thought the voyage would last. All of this would be very expensive.

Christopher and his brother Bartholomew managed to meet several European leaders. Christopher was charming and persuasive, but had a problem convincing any of these leaders to part with their money. Early in 1484 Christopher asked King John II of Portugal to pay for his voyage. But in 1485—the same year Christopher's wife died—the king turned him down.

The king of Portugal and the other European leaders who rejected Columbus's plan were right to do so. Columbus thought that Asia was just 3,000 miles (5,000 km) west of Lisbon and that he could sail there in several weeks. He was wrong. Asia was really over *10,000 miles* (16,000 km) away. And what no European knew was that a huge landmass—North and South America—blocked the path to Asia.

Hundreds of years earlier, in about A.D. 1000, Leif Eriksson had probably become the first European to reach North America. But Eriksson hadn't realized where he had been, and knowledge of his voyage had been lost. Although they didn't know that the Americas blocked the way to Asia, King John II of Portugal

*Leif Eriksson, right, led a Viking
expedition that sighted the coast of
North America about* A.D. *1000.*

and his advisers felt that the world was larger than Columbus did. They turned him down because they thought he and his men would run out of food and water long before reaching Asia.

It was after Christopher's rejection in Portugal that he and Diego sailed south to Spain. They landed in Palos, near Spain's southwestern corner. Christopher knew that the La Rábida monastery near Palos took in students. The father and son walked 4 miles (6 km) to La Rábida, where Diego was accepted as a student. While at La Rábida, Christopher met with the monk Brother Antonio de Marchena, who was interested in astronomy and geography. Impressed by Columbus's idea, Brother Antonio introduced him to the duke of Medina Celi, a wealthy Spanish shipowner.

For a while it seemed that the duke of Medina Celi would pay for Christopher Columbus's dream voyage. Had the duke provided Columbus with ships, men, and supplies in the 1480s, people might have celebrated the 500th anniversary of Columbus's voyage to America in the 1980s instead of having to wait until 1992.

However, the duke realized that for a voyage this important he needed permission from Spain's king and queen. He sent a letter to Queen Isabella, who replied that the duke must not send Columbus out on

*At La Rábida, Columbus worked on plans
for an expedition to find a route to Asia.*

this voyage. Instead, Columbus must visit her and her husband, King Ferdinand. The king and queen wanted the chance to send Christopher Columbus out themselves—if they thought the voyage might be worthwhile.

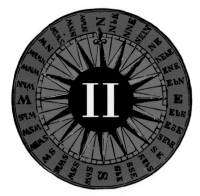

YEARS OF WAITING FOR THE THREE SHIPS

I t was not easy to meet the queen. Nearly a year passed before Christopher Columbus was allowed to speak to her. Apparently, Queen Isabella liked Columbus and his plan. But at the time she and Ferdinand were involved in driving the Muslims out of part of southern Spain and were reluctant to provide all the money Columbus needed for the voyage.

Yet Isabella and Ferdinand did not want Columbus to sail for any other country. If his voyage succeeded, money and glory would come to the nation that sponsored it. The money would come from the trading business that could be built up with Asian lands. The glory would come from the discovery of a new route to Asia. If Columbus were to go at all, Isabella and Ferdinand wanted it to be for them.

Isabella and Ferdinand appointed experts to consider whether the voyage could be made. Since this decision would take time, the rulers provided Columbus with a small salary to live on while he waited.

Years passed as the experts debated whether or not to finance Columbus's voyage. One committee made an unfavorable report in 1490. As with the Portuguese, the Spanish experts correctly thought that the world was larger than Columbus claimed. But Isabella and Ferdinand did not give Columbus a final no. They said they might still decide in his favor once they drove the Muslims out of southern Spain.

One of Columbus's strongest traits was his persistence. Most people would have given up as the years passed, but Columbus explained his idea again and again. And he continued to plan for the day when he would finally hear good news.

The Muslims were driven out of southern Spain in early January of 1492. When he visited Isabella later that month, Columbus was very hopeful. The queen was still sympathetic. However, the king and some of his experts still did not approve of the project. After nearly six years of trying to sell his plan to the royal couple, Columbus seemed to have made no progress.

But the Italian sailor still would not give up. With

the patience of the biblical hero Job, he packed his charts into his saddlebags and climbed onto his mule. He planned to go to France and ask the French king to finance his voyage. But as Christopher Columbus rode away, something remarkable happened. Spain's royal treasurer, Luis de Santangel, spoke to Isabella and convinced the queen that she shouldn't let Columbus sail for another country. Isabella decided to go against her husband and the experts, and even reportedly offered to pawn her jewels if necessary to pay for the voyage.

The queen sent a messenger after Columbus. The messenger found the would-be explorer a few miles down the road and told him the good news. At long last, Christopher Columbus was to receive ships, men, and supplies to make his voyage.

Details of the voyage were worked out in the spring of 1492. Columbus was to have three ships, which we know as the *Niña*, the *Pinta*, and the *Santa María*. These ships were to become three of the most famous sailing vessels in history.

Columbus presented the plans
for his voyage across the sea
to Isabella and Ferdinand,
the rulers of Spain.

Isabella and Ferdinand found a way to limit their costs. Because of a law it had broken, the town of Palos owed the government a fine. Instead of paying in money, the town was ordered to provide two of Columbus's ships.

There were no electric motors in Columbus's time. Oceangoing ships moved when the wind blew against their sails. Earlier in the 1400s, oceangoing vessels called *caravels* had been developed. Caravels were small and fast, yet tough enough to withstand the pounding of ocean waves and wind. Best of all, they were good at moving forward even when the wind wasn't directly behind them. This was done by changing the angle of the sails and the *rudder*, or steering device, in various ways.

Palos provided Columbus with two caravels. In those days, Spanish ships usually had two names, an official name and a nickname that was given to it by its sailors.

One of the caravels that Palos provided was officially called the *Santa Clara*, or "Saint Clara." It is best known by its nickname, the *Niña*. Some experts say it was given that name because it belonged

The caravel was a reliable trading ship of the fifteenth century.

Columbus's fleet was made up of his flagship, the Santa María *(center), and two trading caravels, the* Pinta *and the* Niña.

to the Niño family of the Palos region. Others say it comes from the Spanish word *niña*, or "little girl."

The official name of the second caravel provided by Palos is not known, but it was given the nickname *Pinta*. Some experts think it was given that name because it had once been owned by the Pinto family of Palos. Others think the name comes from the Spanish word *pinta*, or "the painted one."

Columbus's third ship was officially called the *Santa María*, or "Saint Mary." It was a *nao*, a larger and slower ship than a caravel. Columbus chartered the *Santa María* from its owner, Juan de la Cosa, who came from northern Spain. The *Santa María* was nicknamed *La Gallega*, or "the Galician." Galicia is a region of northwestern Spain.

The *Niña*, the *Pinta*, and the *Santa María* were tiny compared to the 1,000-foot (300-m)-long ocean liners of modern times. The *Santa María*, which was the largest but slowest of the three ships, was only about 80 feet (24 m) long—about the size of a long truck. The *Santa María* was Columbus's *flagship*, the one on which he would sail as commander.

The *Pinta*, the fastest of Columbus's three famous ships, was only about 70 feet (21 m) long. The *Niña*, which Columbus considered the most reliable of the vessels, was about the same size as the *Pinta*.

THE CREWS
AND CARGO

Columbus's expedition was scheduled to leave from Palos, Spain, in mid-1492. Recruiting the nearly 100 crew members Columbus needed for his little fleet was not easy. Most sailors were afraid to enter unknown waters. What if Asia was much farther away than Columbus thought? What if they ran out of food and water, or if their vessels were wrecked by storms on the long voyage? And what if sea monsters or other horrors lurked in unknown waters? These were some of the concerns that kept men from signing on as crew members of the *Niña*, the *Pinta*, and the *Santa María*. Columbus had another difficulty to overcome when it came to recruiting men in

*Most portraits of Columbus,
including this one, were drawn
after his death, and so we are not
certain how accurate they are.*

Spain. He was a foreigner, an Italian who had lived in Portugal.

Fortunately, Palos's well-known Pinzón family came to Columbus's rescue. Columbus was to be in overall charge of the expedition and would sail on the flagship, the *Santa María*. However, Vicente Yáñez Pinzón agreed to serve as captain of the *Niña*, and his brother Martín Alonso Pinzón agreed to serve as the *Pinta*'s captain. Since the Pinzóns were willing to sail with Columbus, many other men around Palos decided that they would be, too. Some said that Martín Alonso Pinzón promised the men that they would find houses with golden roofs when they reached Asia.

In all, ninety men, including Columbus, signed up for the expedition. The men who sailed with Columbus were to be paid monthly wages. The *Santa María* would carry forty men, the *Pinta* twenty-six, and the *Niña* twenty-four. Most of the ninety men were sailors. Each ship also had a surgeon; a pilot, who was in charge of the navigation; and a *steward*, who passed out supplies. One of the steward's main

The Santa María *probably looked very much like this drawing that was made in 1493.*

Oceanica Classis

jobs was to make sure that the older foods were passed out first.

Thousands of pounds of supplies were packed into the three ships. The food the men would eat was placed in the ships' holds, or enclosed storage areas. Since there were no refrigerators then, the meat and fish were preserved in salt. Also packed into the holds were sacks of flour and biscuits and various vegetables and fruits, including onions, garlic, olives, figs, and raisins. Water, wine, and oil were carried in barrels.

All the other daily necessities also had to be placed aboard the three ships. These included fuel for fires, candles, dishes, tools, nails, spare wood, and compasses and other navigational instruments. In addition, Columbus brought a supply of glass beads and little bells that he planned to give to the Asians in exchange for their gold. And each man was allowed to bring along a chest containing his personal belongings.

In case the expedition met hostile natives, the ships were armed. They carried cannons called *bom-*

With flags flying, the fleet waited to depart as Columbus and his crew made their farewells.

bards that fired large stones. But the bombards were accurate up to only a couple of hundred feet. Other weapons included smaller guns, crossbows, and swords.

The flagship, the *Santa María*, was equipped with several flags. It flew Queen Isabella's royal flag, which displayed castles and lions. And it flew the expedition's special flag, a green cross with two crowns above the letters F and Y. The F was for Ferdinand, while the Y stood for Isabella in the spelling of those times. As a symbol of Christianity, a red cross was painted on several of the *Santa María*'s sails.

Christopher Columbus also brought along his personal flag, which had a painted image of Jesus Christ on one side and the Virgin Mary on the other. This flag was to be kept in Columbus's cabin, and was to be taken out only on important occasions, such as when they reached land.

THE THREE SHIPS CROSS THE ATLANTIC

The ninety men said good-bye to friends and family on the first two days of August 1492. They then boarded the *Niña*, the *Pinta*, and the *Santa María*. Before dawn of Friday, August 3, the three ships sailed out of Palos.

The ships did not head directly to "Asia." After sailing for over a week, they stopped at Spain's Canary Islands. There the expedition stocked up on food and water. Repairs were also made on the *Pinta*, which was leaking and having rudder problems.

While repairs were being made on the *Pinta*, Columbus changed the *Niña*'s sails. The *Santa María* and the *Pinta* had square sails, but the *Niña* had *lateen*, or triangular, sails. Square sails were better than triangular ones for sailing with the wind, which the ships would be doing on this voyage. Before leaving the Canaries, the *Niña* was provided with square sails like her two sister ships.

The expedition continued on its way from the Canary Islands on September 6. The winds died down for several days, during which the vessels made little progress. Then, on September 9, the wind came up from the east, blowing the ships beyond sight of land that same day. The ninety men on board the three ships would not see land again for over a month.

The *Niña*, the *Pinta*, and the *Santa María* sailed both day and night. Most of the time there were favorable winds from the east that allowed the ships to average about 100 miles (160 km) per day. On some of the best sailing days they were able to travel about 150 miles (240 km).

Unlike Columbus's crew, modern sailors have many tools to help them reach their destinations safely. Precise maps show them where they are going and how to get there. *Gyrocompasses* indicate the exact direction in which they are sailing. Other in-

*Sailing through the day
and night, Columbus guided the ships
due west, into the unknown.*

struments tell them their speed and how far they have gone. Radar helps them avoid bumping into things, and radios keep them in touch with the rest of the world.

Columbus very soon had sailed beyond the edge of the European maps of the known world. Not having modern navigational instruments, he had no way of knowing his speed, the distance traveled, or exactly where he was. However, he did have ways to estimate these.

If you know how fast you are moving and how long you have been going there, you can figure out how far you have traveled. The formula is SPEED × TIME = DISTANCE TRAVELED. For example, if you have been moving in a car for two hours at 50 miles (80 km) per hour, you have gone 100 miles (160 km).

Although there were no clocks aboard the three ships, there were sandglasses, instruments used for measuring time. Each time the sand ran down the glass, another half hour had passed. As for speed, Columbus knew about how fast his ships could go under various conditions. He made an educated guess as to his speed. And by multiplying the speed by the sailing time, he was able to come up with a distance traveled for each day.

Columbus kept two separate records of the dis-

A cross staff was used during Columbus's time to make polestar sightings to help in navigation.

tance traveled. One was his private record of the distance he truly thought they had covered. But Columbus knew that the farther west they went without sighting land, the more fearful his men would become. So he also kept a different record to show the crew. If he thought they had traveled 120 miles (190 km) in a day, he might write it down as 100 miles (160 km) in the record that the crew saw. Actually, he overestimated his ships' speed slightly. The true distance was about halfway between his private record and the one he showed the crew.

To help Columbus determine the direction in which the expedition was sailing, the ships had magnetic compasses. These were not as accurate as our modern gyrocompasses, but were more like the compasses children play with today. Columbus also studied the positions of the stars and the sun to help him roughly determine the ships' position and the direction in which they were headed.

Columbus was very excited to be out at sea after

A reconstruction of Columbus's small cabin in the Santa María *shows the explorer's sword, at left, and the flag of Isabella and Ferdinand under which he sailed.*

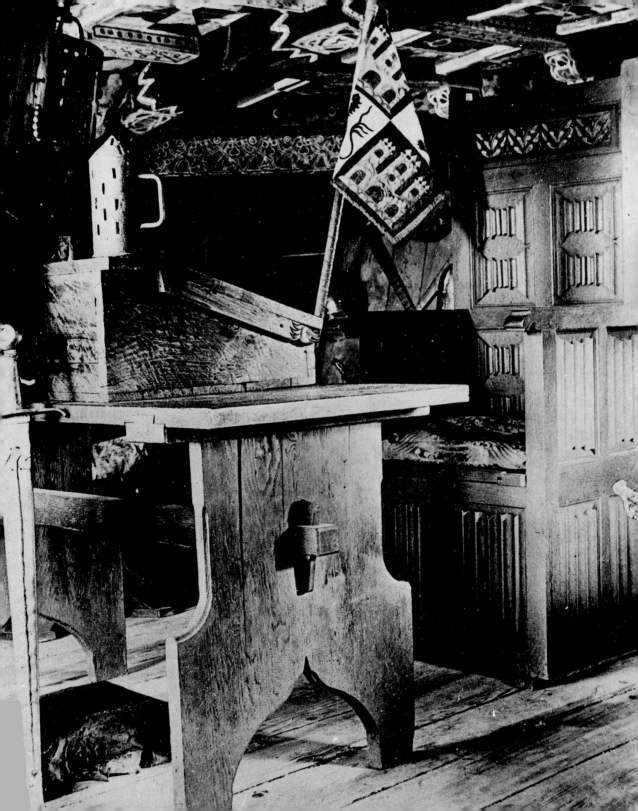

all his years of waiting. His happiness shows in entries he made in his journal. He loved waking up to the smell of the sea so much that he once wrote: "How great a pleasure is the taste of the mornings!"

Columbus had his own cabin on the *Santa María*. In it were a built-in bunk and the desk and chair at which he did his writing. But the other men lived in a great deal of discomfort on the dirty, smelly, crowded, and cockroach-infested ships. Unlike Columbus, the crew had no cabins in which to sleep. Because they were needed on deck in case of emergency, the regular sailors slept in their clothes under the stars. The officers were allowed to sleep in more protected spots, where they kept little bunks or mats.

Cooking was done right out on deck in wood-burning stoves. Since the ships were made of wood, the cooks avoided setting the vessels on fire by spreading dirt or sand under the spot where the cooking was done. This practice inspired a sailors' joke of the time. Sometimes an eager lookout would call out "Land!" but it would prove to be just a cloud on the horizon. When that happened, someone would reply, "You just saw the dirt under the cooking fire!"

The men did some fishing off the ships' decks. The fresh fish they caught were treats compared to the often spoiled food they had brought along. Salting the meat and fish did not do a very good job of preserving those foods. Water turned bad as it sat in

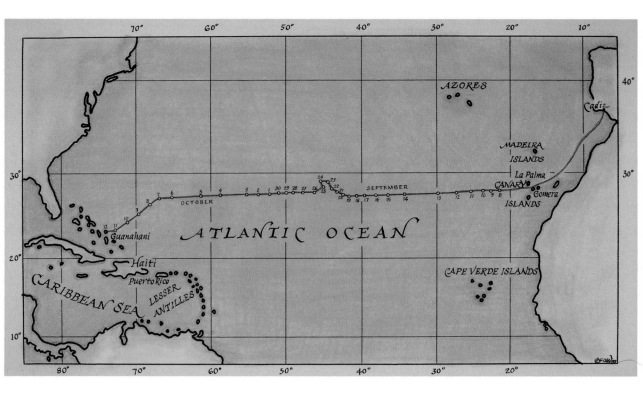

Columbus's first voyage

barrels day after day, and worms got into the biscuits.
Some men kept part of their food until dark so that
they wouldn't see the worms while eating it, but that
didn't take away the smell.

   The three famous ships had no bathrooms. The
men used the ocean as their toilet. While doing so,
they hung on to the *rigging*, or ropes, to keep from
falling into the ocean.

Electric lights weren't invented until the late 1800s—about 400 years after Columbus's historic voyage. Light was produced on the ships with olive-oil lanterns and candles. Because of the danger of fire, only a few lanterns and candles were allowed at night. Columbus had a light in his cabin so he could work on his charts and journal. There was also a lantern carried at the rear of each ship to warn other vessels of its presence. And there was a light that illuminated the compass.

Most of the men went to sleep at nightfall. Only those in charge of sailing the ships and those who served as lookouts stayed awake. On clear nights, the lookouts could see quite well by the light of the moon or the stars.

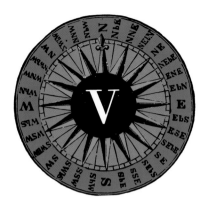

"I SHALL SAIL ON!"

Day after day passed with no sign of land. Several times the men *thought* they had seen land, but it proved to be clouds. As the days turned into weeks, the men became terrified. They wondered if they would ever reach Asia. And even if they did, would they be able to find their way back home?

By late September many of the crew wanted to turn back. Some even spoke to Christopher Columbus about it. But Columbus, who rarely seemed to feel any fear, refused to turn around. "There is no point in your complaining," he told one group that asked him to head home. "I am going to the Indies [Asia] and I shall sail on until, with God's help, I find them."

Some of the crew probably thought Columbus was

crazy. There may even have been plots to *mutiny*, or overthrow Columbus. The one thing protecting Columbus was the fact that he was the best sailor in the expedition. The others knew they might not be able to find their way home without him.

On October 7, flocks of birds flew over the ships. The birds were heading a little south of west. Columbus knew that the birds were probably flying toward land. He changed course a little to the south to follow the birds. Two days later, land had still not been sighted. Realizing that the men were close to mutiny, Columbus compromised with them on October 9 or 10. If they did not reach land within three days, they would return to Spain.

On October 11, there were a few signs of land, including branches and a carved stick that floated past their ships. At ten that night, Columbus thought he saw a dim light to the west. Perhaps it was wishful thinking on Columbus's part, or perhaps he saw a fire made by Indians on an island they were approaching. Then, at two o'clock on the morning of October 12, 1492, the *Pinta*'s lookout made a definite sighting of

A nineteenth-century artist shows Columbus's weary and frightened crew threatening to mutiny.

*The frigate, or man-of-war,
bird sighted crossing the sky
was a sign of land.*

land. *"Tierra! Tierra!"* or "Land! Land!" he called. They had reached one of the islands known as the Bahamas, off Florida's southeast coast. The exact island they had reached is still debated.

The men did not leave the ships that first night. But in the morning, Christopher Columbus, Captain Vicente Yáñez Pinzón, and Captain Martín Alonso Pinzón went ashore. Columbus claimed the land for Spain. And, thinking he was in the Indies, or Asia, he named the friendly people he met *"Indians."*

Columbus and his men spent about three months in the New World. While looking for gold, they explored not only the Bahamas but also Cuba and Hispaniola, the island on which the present-day countries of Haiti and the Dominican Republic are located. Columbus did not realize that he had reached the Americas, which lie between Europe and Asia. He thought he was in the region of China and Japan. Something about the Indians puzzled Columbus, however. Why didn't they have the treasures and the type of villages that were said to exist in Asia?

While the three ships were exploring, Martín Alonso Pinzón sailed the *Pinta* away from the other two ships to look for gold, an act that angered Columbus. On December 24, 1492, something even worse happened. While sailing in hazardous waters, Columbus usually stayed up all night and remained

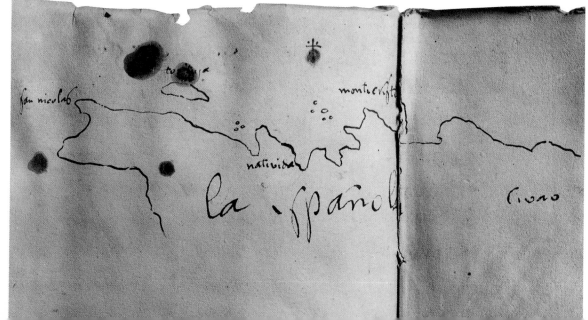

la spañola

fan nicolab   to...a   montecrifti   natiuidad   tiano

on the *Santa María*'s deck. But because he had slept very little for forty-eight hours, he went to bed in his cabin on that Christmas Eve.

The *Santa María*'s *helmsman*, or person who steers the ship, was also very tired, and as a result did something that was forbidden. He went to sleep, leaving a young boy in charge of the steering. The boy soon steered the ship off course and onto a reef near the coast of present-day Haiti.

The boy let out a yell, bringing Columbus and a few other men out on deck within seconds. Christopher Columbus tried to save the *Santa María*, but the reef began to tear at the ship's bottom. Sadly, Columbus had to order his men to abandon his flagship. The *Pinta* was still off on its own, and the *Niña* was too small to carry all the *Santa María*'s men. Because

Top, left: As the sun rose on October 12, 1492, Columbus and his crew rejoiced at the sight of land.

Bottom, left: Columbus sketched a map of the northwest coast of Hispaniola, noting his arrival at a place he named San Nicolas. To the east is the area called Natividad where he later ordered a settlement built, and the mountain (right) he named Montecristo. The black splotches on the map are inkspots from Columbus's pen.

*Grounded on a coral reef and
battered by the ocean's swelling
waves, the* Santa María *sank off
the coast of Hispaniola.*

of this, Columbus decided to leave forty men behind
on Haiti to hunt for gold and build a settlement.

Several days later, Columbus, now aboard the
Niña, sighted the *Pinta*. Martín Alonso Pinzón was
so popular among the men that Columbus was afraid
to punish him for having sailed off on his own. In mid-
January 1493 the two ships headed back together toward Spain.

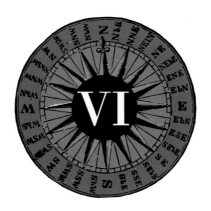

THE TRIP HOME

Columbus and his men had one advantage on their return trip. They knew exactly where they wanted to go—home to Spain. But despite that, the homeward voyage was more difficult than the passage to America had been. The two vessels ran into storms. On the night of February 13 the ships were separated in a storm.

Columbus was so worried that the *Niña* would sink that on St. Valentine's Day, February 14, 1493 he wrote a report about his voyage. He placed the report in an empty cask that he then threw overboard, hoping that it would wash onto a beach and be found. This report, which would be incredibly valuable today, has never been found and may still be somewhere in the Atlantic Ocean. But, thanks to the fine construction of the ships and the great work by their crews, the *Niña* and the *Pinta* made it back to Palos, Spain, on March 15, 1493.

A hero's welcome awaited Columbus in Spain. He had brought proof of his visit to a distant place—some Indians he had kidnapped and a little gold. People from all across Spain's countryside came to cheer Columbus and stare at the Indians as they walked to the court of Ferdinand and Isabella.

The queen and king hailed Columbus as a great hero, too, and heaped many honors on him. They also sent him on three more voyages to start colonies in the islands he had discovered and to bring home gold.

Columbus made three more trips to the "Other World," as he called the Americas. He never did understand the true nature of this "Other World." To his dying day, he apparently believed that he had visited the outskirts of Asia.

Although Columbus had not been the first European to reach the New World, he was the first to begin colonizing it. The group of sailors he had left on Haiti were killed after they mistreated the Indians. But on his later voyages, Columbus helped start other colonies in the islands off the southeastern coast of the present-day United States. Columbus never did reach the mainland of what is now the United States. But because his famous voyage of 1492 led to Euro-

*At a great celebration in the royal court
in Barcelona, Isabella and Ferdinand
welcomed Columbus, followed by crew
members and a group of captive Indians.*

pean colonization of the Americas, people in the United States and parts of Latin America honor him by celebrating Columbus Day each October.

Columbus's last three voyages to the Americas were unhappy for both the Indians and the great explorer. Unfortunately, Columbus had begun enslaving the Indians by kidnapping a few of them on his first voyage. After that, the Spaniards captured many thousands of Indians and forced them to work as their slaves. Thousands of these Indians struggled against slavery and were killed.

As for the great explorer, he proved to be very poor at running colonies. In fact, Christopher Columbus ran the Spanish colony on the island of Hispaniola so poorly that he was sent home from his third voyage in chains. Isabella and Ferdinand released him, however, and sent him on one more voyage. During this last trip to the New World, Columbus was marooned on Jamaica for a year, an experience that ruined his health. The world's most famous explorer died on May 20, 1506, less than two years after returning from his fourth and last voyage.

And what of the three famous ships? The *Santa María* had been lost on a reef during the first voyage. The *Niña*, which Columbus especially loved, was part of his fleet on both his second and third voyages. In October of 1499 the *Niña* was sold. The last that

*In October 1500, Columbus was sent
back to Spain in chains.*

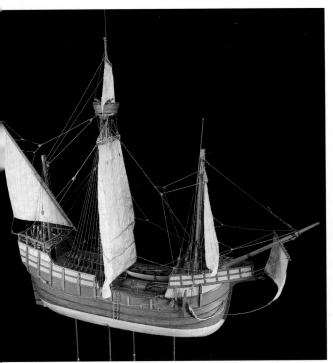

Model reconstructions of the
Santa María *(left) and the* Pinta

seems to be known about the *Niña* was a voyage she
made to Africa in 1501. The *Pinta* made no more
voyages for Columbus after the famous first one, and
what became of her is a mystery. However, the names
of the three ships will be honored for as long as there
are people in the Americas. For with them Christopher Columbus opened up a "New World" to Europeans while searching for a better route to Asia.

GLOSSARY

Astronomy—the study of stars, planets, and other heavenly bodies.

Bombard—a cannon that fires large stones.

Caravel—a small, fast ship of long ago.

Colony—a settlement built by a people who are from another country.

Compass—a device used for determining direction.

Expedition—a journey with a special purpose.

Flagship—the ship on which the commander sails and which flies the expedition's main flags.

Gyrocompass—a modern type of compass that is more accurate than the magnetic compasses used by Columbus.

Helmsman—the person who steers a ship.

Hold—the enclosed storage area of a ship.

Lateen—a type of triangular sail.

Monastery—a place where men who have taken religious vows live.

Mutiny—to revolt, especially aboard a ship.

Nao—a Spanish word meaning "ship"; a *nao* referred to a large type of vessel in Columbus's time.

Rigging—the ropes and chains of a sailing vessel.

Rudder—a steering device for a ship or airplane.

Steward—a person on a ship who is in charge of food and supplies.

FOR FURTHER READING

Fradin, Dennis Brindell. *Columbus Day*. Hillside, N.J.: Enslow Publishers, 1990.

Fradin, Dennis Brindell. *Explorers: A New True Book*. Chicago: Children's Press, 1984.

Levinson, Nancy Smiler. *Christopher Columbus: Voyager to the Unknown*. New York: Dutton, 1990.

Lomask, Milton. *Great Lives: Exploration*. New York: Scribners, 1988.

Martinez-Hidalgo, José Maria. *Columbus' Ships*. Barre, Mass.: Barre Publishers, 1966.

Soule, Gardner. *Christopher Columbus on the Green Sea of Darkness*. New York: Franklin Watts, 1988.

Ventura, Piero. *Christopher Columbus*. New York: Random House, 1978.

INDEX